THE POWER

of

DISCIPLINE & DEDICATION

"But I keep under my body,
and bring it into subjection:
lest that by any means, when
I have preached to others, I
myself should be a castaway."

1Cor9:26

by

Franklin N. Abazie

The power of discipline & dedication
COPYRIGHT 2019 BY Franklin N Abazie
ISBN: 978:1-945-133-848

All right reserved. This book or any portion thereof may be reproduced or used in any manner whatsoever without the express written permission of the publisher, except for the use of brief quotations in a book review. All Bible quotes are from King James Version and others as noted.

Published by:
F N ABAZIE PUBLISHING HOUSE-a.k.a,
Empowerment Bookstore:

That I may publish with the voice of thanksgiving and tell of all thy wondrous works.
Psalms26:7

To order additional copies, wholesales or booking:
Call the Church office (973-372-7518)
or Empowerment Bookstore Hotline 973-393-8518

Worship address:
343 Sanford Avenue Newark New Jersey 07106
Administrative Head Office address:
33 Schley Street Newark New Jersey 07112
Email:pastorfranknto@yahoo.com
Website www.fnabaziehealingministries.org
Publishing House: www.fnabaziepublishinghouse.org

This book is a production of F N Abazie Publishing House. A publication Arms of Miracle of God Ministries 2019
First Edition

CONTENTS

THE MANDATE OF THE COMMISSION iv

FAVOR CONFESSION vi

INTRODUCTION viii

CHAPTER 1:
The Power of Discipline & Hard-Work 40

CHAPTER 2
The Power of Dedication & Focus 57

CHAPTER 3
Prayer of Salvation 81

CHAPTER 4
About The Author 92

Books by Rev Franklin N Abazie 95

The Power of Discipline & Dedication

THE MANDATE OF THE COMMISSION

"THE MOMENT IS DUE TO IMPACT YOUR WORLD THROUGH THE REVIVAL OF THE HEALING & MIRACLE MINISTRY OF JESUS CHRIST OF NAZARETH."

"I AM SENDING YOU TO RESTORE HEALTH UNTO THEE AND I WILL HEAL THEE OF THY WOUNDS, SAID THE LORD OF HOST."

ARMS OF THE COMMISSION

1) F N Abazie Ministries-Miracle of God Ministries (Miracle Chapel Intl)
2) F N Abazie TV Ministries: Global Television Ministry Outreach.
3) F N Abazie Radio Ministries: Radio Broadcasting Outreach.
4) F N Abazie Publishing House: Book Publication.
5) F N Abazie Bible School: also called Word of Healing Bible School (W.O.H.B.S)
6) F N Abazie Evangelistic Ass: Miracle of God Ministries: Global Crusade
7) Empowerment Bookstore: Book distribution.
8) F N Abazie Helping Hands: Meeting the help of the needy world wide
9) F N Abazie Disaster Recovery Mission: Global Disaster Recovery.
10) F N Abazie Prison Ministry: Prison Ministry for all convicts "Second chance"

Some of our ministry arms are waiting the appointed time to commence.

The Power of Discipline & Dedication

FAVOR CONFESSION

Father thank you for making me righteous and accepted through the blood of Jesus Christ. Because of that, I am blessed and highly favored by God. I am the subject of your affection. Your favor surrounds me as a shield, and the first thing that people see around me is your favored shield.

Thank you that I have favor with you and man today. All day long people go out of their way to bless me and help me. I have favor with everyone that I deal with today. Doors that were once closed are now opened for me. I receive preferential treatment, and I have special privileges, I am Gods favored child.

No good thing will he withhold from me. Because of Gods favor my enemies cannot triumph over my life. I have supernatural increase and promotion. I declare restoration to everything that the devil has

Favor Confession

stolen from my life. I have honor in the midst of my adversaries and an increase in assets, especially in real estate and expansion of territories.

Because I am highly favored by God, I experience great victories, supernatural turnarounds, and miraculous breakthrough in the midst of great impossibilities. I receive recognition, prominence, and honor. Petitions are granted to me even by ungodly authorities. Policies, rules, regulations, and laws are changed and reverse on my behalf.

I win battles that I don't even have to fight, because God fights them for me. This is the day, the set time and the designated moment for me to experience the free favor of God, that profusely and lavishly abound on my behalf in Jesus name. **Amen.**

INTRODUCTION

"And Solomon determined to build an house for the name of the Lord, and an house for his kingdom." **1chronicle2:2**

"Discipline is the soul of an army. It makes small numbers formidable; procures success to the weak, and esteem to all."
--George Washington

As believers, we must be discipline with our time, business, money, and people. If you have do not a disciplined character, *your skill, and gift will not take you far in life*. Your skill and talent will take you far in life, but it will take *a disciplined* character to attain be successful in life.

Discipline and dedication is all we need to succeed in life. Pele the great once said *"Success is no accident. It is hard work, perseverance, learning, studying, sacrifice*

Introduction

and most of all, love of what you are doing or learning to do."-**Pele**

This small book is a book of wisdom and success. I have written this book for those of us that desire to succeed in life. Although hard work pays in life, it is discipline that will allow you to enjoy the blessing of God upon your life.

"According as his divine power hath given unto us all things that pertain unto life and godliness, through the knowledge of him that hath called us to glory and virtue." **2Peter1:3**

In this book you will discover that it takes discipline and dedication to overcome the obstacles in our life. It also takes discipline to breakthrough in life. *Although talent and skill you will help you succeed in life, it will take character and discipline to preserve your success.* Come with me let's hear what God is saying about discipline in life. Happy Reading!

HIS DESTINY WAS THE CROSS....

HIS PURPOSE WAS LOVE....

HIS REASON WAS YOU....

"Whoever loves discipline loves knowledge, but he who hates reproof is stupid."

Proverb12:1

As many as I love, I rebuke and chasten: be zealous therefore, and repent.

Rev 3:19

> "I therefore so run,
> not as uncertainly;
> so fight I, not as one
> that beateth the air:"
> **1cor9:26**

"But I keep under my body, and bring it into subjection: lest that by any means, when I have preached to others, I myself should be a castaway."

1cor9:27

"I must work the works of him that sent me, while it is day: the night cometh, when no man can work."

John9:4

"Whoever spares the rod hates his son, but he who loves him is diligent to discipline him."

Proverb13:24

"Those whom I love, I reprove and discipline, so be zealous and repent."

Revelation 3:19

"The rod and reproof give wisdom, but a child left to himself brings shame to his mother."

Proverb29:15

"So he fed them
according to the
integrity of his heart;
and guided them
by the skilfulness
of his hands."

Psalm 78:72

"And ye have forgotten the exhortation which speaketh unto you as unto children, My son, despise not thou the chastening of the Lord, nor faint when thou art rebuked of him:"

Hebrews12:5

"For whom the Lord loveth he chasteneth, and scourgeth every son whom he receiveth."

Hebrews12:6

"If ye endure chastening, God dealeth with you as with sons; for what son is he whom the father chasteneth not"?

Hebrews12:7

"But if ye be without chastisement, whereof all are partakers, then are ye bastards, and not sons."

Hebrews12:8

"Furthermore we have had fathers of our flesh which corrected us, and we gave them reverence: shall we not much rather be in subjection unto the Father of spirits, and live?"

Hebrews12:9

"He that spareth his rod hateth his son: but he that loveth him chasteneth him betimes."

Proverb13:24

"Let thy work appear unto thy servants, and thy glory unto their children."

Psalm 90:16

"And let the beauty of the Lord our God be upon us: and establish thou the work of our hands upon us; yea, the work of our hands establish thou it."

Psalm 90:17

"And he shall be like a tree planted by the rivers of water, that bringeth forth his fruit in his season; his leaf also shall not wither; and whatsoever he doeth shall prosper."

Psalm 1:3

"I must work the works of him that sent me, while it is day: the night cometh, when no man can work."

John9:4

"For even when we were with you, this we commanded you, that if any would not work, neither should he eat."

2theo3:10

"And that ye study to be quiet, and to do your own business, and to work with your own hands, as we commanded you;

1theo4:11

"To discipline a child produces wisdom, but a mother is disgraced by an undisciplined child."

Proverbs 29:15

"Whoever loves discipline loves knowledge, but whoever hates correction is stupid."

Proverbs 12:1

"Blessed is the one whom God corrects; so do not despise the discipline of the Almighty."

Job 5:17

"Blessed is the one you discipline, LORD, the one you teach from your law;"
Psalm 94:12

But Jesus answered them, My Father worketh hitherto, and I work.
John 5:17

THE REWARD OF DISCIPLINE AND DEDICATION IN LIFE

As long as you make up your mind to be disciplined and dedicated, the sky is your limit. *You can never fail in life living a discipline and dedicated life.* There is a great reward for every disciplined and dedicated man and woman. *Successful men and women are disciplined and dedicated people in life.*

To be great, you must be a man or woman with a disciplined character. That is- you must behave well. Every discipline man and woman are men who can see their future in advance.

For you to succeed in life, you have to plan ahead, prepare ahead, and expect to succeed ahead of your future. A man or woman of great reputation. *"The integrity of the upright shall guide them: but the perverseness of transgressors shall destroy them."* **Proverb11:3**

Character is the will-power to do what's right in the midst of great trials, temptation, and difficulty in life. So many of us desire to be the best in life, but lack the concentration, and attention to details to accomplish it

If you want to be successful in life you must be faithful, diligent, dedicated, devoted, disciplined, focused, and work hard. Some people believe in good luck, I want you to believe in God for hard-work. I believe we must all earn whatever we deserve in life.

The Holy bible says…

"Let thy work appear unto thy servants, and thy glory unto their children." **Psalm 90:16**

"And let the beauty of the Lord our God be upon us: and establish thou the work of our hands upon us; yea, the work of our hands establish thou it." **Psalm90:17**

"And he shall be like a tree planted by the rivers of water, that bringeth forth his fruit in his season; his leaf also shall not wither; and whatsoever he doeth shall prosper." **Psalm1:3**

"I must work the works of him that sent me, while it is day: the night cometh, when no man can work." **John9:4**

"For even when we were with you, this we commanded you, that if any would not work, neither should he eat." **2theo3:10**

"And that ye study to be quiet, and to do your own business, and to work with your own hands, as we commanded you;" **1theo4:11**

CHAPTER 1
THE POWER OF DISCIPLINE & HARD-WORK

"I therefore so run, not as uncertainly; so fight I, not as one that beateth the air:" **1cor9:26**

"But I keep under my body, and bring it into subjection: lest that by any means, when I have preached to others, I myself should be a castaway." **1cor9:27**

"But Jesus answered them, My Father worketh hitherto, and I work." **John5:17**

"I must work the works of him that sent me, while it is day: the night cometh, when no man can work." **John9:4**

Despite any opposition that may confront us in life, discipline combined with

Chapter 1 : The Power of Discipline & Hard-Work

hard-work will make any dummy succeed in life. *Discipline is the key to success in life.* In any disciplined man or woman you will always find *determination*. A zeal to succeed despite prevailing challenges in life. *Discipline is a product of love.* Whatever you love to do in life, you must be *disciplined to be hardworking.*

Whether it is God's discipline, self-discipline, child discipline, or character discipline, *you cannot emerge high flyer*, or great in life without the power of discipline in your life. For an example, everyone elected into any office in America government, always go through some screerning examination about their character, morals, and level of discipline in life. Whenever we think of discipline think of love. It is love that begets discipline in life. *"As many as I love, I rebuke and chasten: be zealous therefore, and repent."* **Rev3:19**

The Power of Discipline & Dedication

"Discipline must begin with the body for every true Christian. Discipline will help us present our body as a living sacrifice. "I beseech you therefore, brethren, by the mercies of God, that ye present your bodies a living sacrifice, holy, acceptable unto God, which is your reasonable service." **Romans12:1**

So many people have missed this. I pray you will not miss it in your life. David said *"So he fed them according to the integrity of his heart; and guided them by the skilfulness of his hands."* **Psalm78:72.**

"What? know ye not that your body is the temple of the Holy Ghost which is in you, which ye have of God, and ye are not your own?" **1cor6:19**

"Know ye not that ye are the temple of God, and that the Spirit of God dwelleth in you?" **1cor3:16**

Chapter 1 : The Power of Discipline & Hard-Work

"If any man defile the temple of God, him shall God destroy; for the temple of God is holy, which temple ye are." **1cor3:17**

"We cannot give our hearts to God and keep our bodies for ourselves." **Elisabeth Elliot**

"We may feel God's hand as a Father upon us when He strikes us as well as when He strokes us." **Abraham Wright**

Although talent and skill will make anyone to be rich and successful in life. But it will take discipline of your character to keep you safe and free from problem"
"But I keep under my body, and bring it into subjection: lest that by any means, when I have preached to others, I myself should be a castaway." **1cor9:27**

I have witnessed great medical doctor's end their life in shame and in jail because they lacked the moral character to sustain their success in life. I have also seen great sports athletes, end up broke, and go to jail, I have also seen heavy weight boxing champions, great musicians, and powerful politicians all end up in shame and in jail because they lacked the moral character that comes from a disciplined life to stay out of trouble, and immorality in life. *"He that hath no rule over his own spirit is like a city that is broken down, and without walls."* **Proverb 25:28**

"He that spareth his rod hateth his son: but he that loveth him chasteneth him betimes." **Proverb 13:24**

"My son, despise not the chastening of the Lord; neither be weary of his correction: For whom the Lord loveth he correcteth; even as a father the son in whom he delighteth." **Proverb 3:11-12**

We were told for "For God so loved the world that he gave his only begotten Son,

Chapter 1 : The Power of Discipline & Hard-Work

that whosoever believeth in him should not perish, but have everlasting life." **John3:16**

God's discipline helps us make the right decision in life

It's difficult to make the right decision in life especially when you are possessed by the *vain glory of life*. Some people forget about *discipline* once money is rolling into their life. *Remember... money is the root of all evil.* Often some folks forget the power of the law of the land. No one is above the laws of God and the moral law of life. If you commit a crime you must do the time.

Often in Africa, and other third world countries, rich folks try to buy their freedom by bribing corrupt law enforcement officials. In the eyes of God you cannot bribe God with anything. I admonish you to develop the power of discipline. To practice righteousness and live right with all men. *"And herein do I exercise myself, to have always a conscience void to offence toward God, and toward men."* **Acts 24:16**

"And Paul, earnestly beholding the council, said, Men, and brethren, I have lived in all good conscience before God until this day." **Acts 23:1**

God's discipline is the foundation for Repentance.

Often God will discipline us through the challenges and obstacle opposing us in life. Some of us are very stubborn and must learn the hard way. "Before I was afflicted I went astray: but now have I kept thy word." **Psalm 119:67**

"It is good for me that I have been afflicted; that I might learn thy statutes." **Psalm 119:71**

Self-discipline is a self-imposed standard; a restriction motivated by a desire than the alternative. It is doing what is

Chapter 1 : The Power of Discipline & Hard-Work

demanded not convenient. Self-discipline is created by a power of the mind in distinguishing choices in life. Some people will settle for anything. But a discipline person will make a concise choice and stick with it. *"He that hath no rule over his own spirit is like a city that is broken down, and without walls."* **Proverb25:28**

Self-discipline means developing a set standard for one's self. That means you set a boundary and parameter for yourself; you can never be great deceiving yourself. To be the best, you must be disciplined with your time, resources, conversations, reading habit, associations, music you listen to, and what you watch. Discipline yourself to the demand of what you want to be.

Never follow the crowd if you want the crowd to follow you; follow God. That everybody is doing it does not mean you should do it. When you do anyhow, your life will be anyhow. When liberty lacks control, it becomes captivity. Either you receive the pain of today to become great tomorrow or you play today to be in pain tomorrow. Some short term gains can cost you long term pains.

To be self-disciplined, the ability to manage time is very important. Time is one of the greatest assets God gave man. It is perishable, irretrievable, and irreplaceable. Once it is gone or wasted, you cannot recover it. Time management is the ability to choose the sequence of events; always apply the ABCDE of time.

A – What I must do

B – What I should do

C – Things that are nice to do but are not necessary

D – Things to delegate

E – Things to eliminate

Chapter 1 : The Power of Discipline & Hard-Work

These principle will help you in time management when planning the day, and also realize that there are common time wasters which are:

1. Telephone

2. Paperwork

3. Social media

4. Unnecessary meeting: People who hold too many meetings don't achieve too many things.

5. Visitors: Program your life when you receive visitors.

Be self-disciplined even with your money and clothes. The first and best victory to become great is to conquer self.

Samson conquered everybody but didn't conquer himself so Delilah did.

Judas conquered everybody except himself so money conquered him. Conquer yourself first, have self-discipline, and watch yourself grow to greatness!

THINGS MENTALLY STRONG PEOPLE DO

1) They enjoy their time with their family and create time for meditation

2) They hold themselves accountable for their actions

3) They celebrate the success of others.

4) They surround themselves with greatness.

5) They have great health habits. That is from sleep to the choices of food they eat.

6) They rule their world-They make decisions and do not seek others opinion.

7) They own their mind, body, and spirit.

Chapter 1 : The Power of Discipline & Hard-Work

8) They embrace and celebrate change.

9) They are readers and life learners.

10) They know that change is constant.

11) They invest time and energy into the present.

12) They are able to focus to accomplish any task

13) They do not make excuses.

14) They confront challenges.

15) They see opportunities in obstacles

16) They make their money well.

17) They take advantage of the least opportunity in life

The Power of Discipline & Dedication

Children must be discipline

"Withhold not correction from the child: for if thou beatest him with the rod, he shall not die." **Proverb23:13**

"Thou shalt beat him with the rod, and shalt deliver his soul from hell." **Proverb23:14**

"Foolishness is bound in the heart of a child; but the rod of correction shall drive it far from him." **Proverb22:15**

Every child must be disciplined. *Otherwise you will regret if that child grows up to become a man without the virtues of a disciplined-ordered life.* When God disciplines us He does not intend to kill us. Likewise we should do to our children. *"Chasten thy son while there is hope, and let not thy soul spare for his crying."* **Proverb19:18**

Chapter 1 : The Power of Discipline & Hard-Work

How does God chasten us?

You have to understand that God is spirit. *"God is a Spirit: and they that worship him must worship him in spirit and in truth."* **John4:24**

The way God disciplines us is completely different from the way we suppose or expect it to happen. *"For my thoughts are not your thoughts, neither are your ways my ways, saith the Lord. For as the heavens are higher than the earth, so are my ways higher than your ways, and my thoughts than your thoughts."* **Isaiah55:8-9**

God will discipline us through hardship, and challenges in life, sickness, lack of peace, or through any negative means that you least expect. *"For God speaketh once, yea twice, yet man perceiveth it not. In a dream, in a vision of the night, when deep sleep falleth upon men, in slumberings upon the bed; Then he openeth the ears of men, and sealeth their instruction."* **Job33:14-16**

You may ask me… Does God give trouble?

It is written…

"Man that is born of a woman is of few days and full of trouble." **Job14:1**

"I form the light, and create darkness: I make peace, and create evil: I the Lord do all these things." **Isaiah45:7**

"The Lord killeth, and maketh alive: he bringeth down to the grave, and bringeth up." **1samuel2:6**

"The Lord maketh poor, and maketh rich: he bringeth low, and lifteth up." **1samuel2:7**

Perhaps God have dealth with you in a way that even as you read this book, you

Chapter 1 : The Power of Discipline & Hard-Work

still doubt if that was the devil or God. God disciplines us daily.

"For whom the Lord loveth he chasteneth, and scourgeth every son whom he receiveth. If ye endure chastening, God dealeth with you as with sons; for what son is he whom the father chasteneth not? But if ye be without chastisement, whereof all are partakers, then are ye bastards, and not sons. Furthermore we have had fathers of our flesh which corrected us, and we gave them reverence: shall we not much rather be in subjection unto the Father of spirits, and live? For they verily for a few days chastened us after their own pleasure; but he for our profit, that we might be partakers of his holiness. Now no chastening for the present seemeth to be joyous, but grievous: nevertheless afterward it yieldeth the peaceable fruit of righteousness unto them which are exercised thereby. Wherefore lift

up the hands which hang down, and the feeble knees; And make straight paths for your feet, lest that which is lame be turned out of the way; but let it rather be healed." **Hebrews 12:6-1**

CHAPTER 2
THE POWER OF DEDICATION & FOCUS

"Verily, verily, I say unto you, Except a corn of wheat fall into the ground and die, it abideth alone: but if it die, it bringeth forth much fruit."
John 12:24

"And Jesus said unto him, No man, having put his hand to the plough, and looking back, is fit for the kingdom of God." **Luke 9:62**

It takes dedication, and focus to survive in this era that we live in. It will take discipline, dedication, devotion, focus, and hard work for every believer to succeed in this technology age that we live in.

The Power of Discipline & Dedication

If every one of us can capture this key (dedication, & focus) to succeed in life, every believer will walk out cheaply on poverty, shame, and begging. My point is no Christian should solely depend on prayer alone. It is awesome to pray and believe in God. But every time you pray you must take concrete action towards actualization your goals in life. The power of dedication and focus literally means:

1) Focus means paying attention to one thing alone.

"And Jesus said unto him, No man, having put his hand to the plough, and looking back, is fit for the kingdom of God."**Luke9:62**

Do you want to succeed in life? Then you must pay attention to details. You but be discipline to focus on one thing in life.

2) Concentrating all your energy on one particular thing.

Chapter 2 : The Power of Dedication & Focus

3) For unless you specialize on one thing alone in life , it is difficult to succeed. David said *"One thing have I desired of the Lord, that will I seek after; that I may dwell in the house of the Lord all the days of my life, to behold the beauty of the Lord, and to enquire in his temple."* **Psalm27:4**

4) Focus means being driven by a purpose in life.

What are the thing you love to do in life? **Are you driven by a purpose?** Catch a vision from the Lord and May you concentrate on one thing alone in life.

"Brethren, I count not myself to have apprehended: but this one thing I do, forgetting those things which are behind, and reaching forth unto those things which are before, I press toward the mark for the prize of the high calling of God in Christ Jesus." **Phil3:13-14**

5) The Power of planning.

Planning is the foundation for purpose in life. *If you have not planned to succeed, you have planned to fail.* "For which of you, intending to build a tower, sitteth not down first, and counteth the cost, whether he have sufficient to finish it?" **Luke14:28**

Planning will deliver you from frustration, from lack, from begging, from shame and reproach. Child of God there must be a plan in your life others you have planned to fail. I pray you plan your life to succeed in Jesus Name.

If you will plan ahead, and plan well in life, you have laid the corner stone of success in life. If you can see ahead, plan ahead, you will get ahead in life. *One man said "men are in seizes, but life is in phases."*

Are you a man or woman with a vision from the Lord? Then you must develop the following qualities in life:

Chapter 2 : The Power of Dedication & Focus

DEDICATION

Have you discovered God's plan for your life? If so then dedicate yourself to what God has called you to do in life.

"For I would that all men were even as I myself. But every man hath his proper gift of God, one after this manner, and another after that." **1cor7:7**

"But as God hath distributed to every man, as the Lord hath called every one, so let him walk. And so ordain I in all churches." **1cor7:17**

"Let every man abide in the same calling wherein he was called."**1cor7:20**

"Brethren, let every man, wherein he is called, therein abide with God." **1cor7:24**

We must put all our energy in the assignment God has called you to do in life. "And Jesus said unto him, No man, having put his hand to the plough, and looking back, is fit for the kingdom of God." We must be ready to give it all it takes to accomplish any task God has given you to do in life.

"Verily, verily, I say unto you, Except a corn of wheat fall into the ground and die, it abideth alone: but if it die, it bringeth forth much fruit." John12:24

The above scripture says except a corn of wheat fall into the gropund and die, it abideth alone; but if it die, it bringeth forth much fruit. *Are you ready to die to a cause?* For unless you are ready to sacrifice whatever it takes to train, to learn, to do what God has called you to do, you will not succeed in life. But I see you succeeding in the midst of challenges in life.

Chapter 2 : The Power of Dedication & Focus

DETERMINATION

In 1986, I heard that determination is the key to success. If you are determined, you will succeed. It's just a question of time. "Be determined in life" Determination is all it take to emerge successful in life. *A dream doesn't become reality through magic; it takes sweat, determination, and hard work.*

Don't bother people for help without first trying to solve the problem yourself. I see you succeeding in the midst of great impossibilities. Jesus is Lord!

DEVOTION

I cannot over emphasize it again; you must be devoted to your work. You must embrace your God given assignment and put all your positive energy into it. There are no secrets to success. It is the result of preparation, hard work, and learning from failure.

The Power of Discipline & Dedication

HARD WORK

If Jesus said I must work **"I must work the works of him that sent me, while it is day: the night cometh, when no man can work." John9:4**

"But Jesus answered them, My Father worketh hitherto, and I work." **John5:17**

What are you doing without a job?

"Whatsoever thy hand findeth to do, do it with thy might; for there is no work, nor device, nor knowledge, nor wisdom, in the grave, whither thou goest." **Eccl9:10**

Hardwork is not cheap. It takes courage to be productive in life. If anyone must succeed, they must become a "hard worker". Success is the result of perfection, hard work, learning from failure, loyalty, and persistence. We must therefore surround ourselves with people who are diligent, dedicated, and take their work very serious.

Chapter 2 : The Power of Dedication & Focus

FOCUS

"And Jesus said unto him, No man, having put his hand to the plough, and looking back, is fit for the kingdom of God." **Luke9:62**

If you do not know where you are going, everywhere will look like you destination. Focus has power to uproot all the unnecessary distraction that the devil planted along your path to greatness. You will never become great in life without the power of focus. Focus is all it takes to be attentive and to be informed.

God is reminding you to be focus. Be diligent. Be patient, be humble. Be hard working, be honest, and be truthful. I see your life changing finally. I see you moving to your next level in life. I see you breaking through strong hold s and barriers.

The Power of Discipline & Dedication

I want to hear from you.

Take time and write me:

Rev Franklin N Abazie
33 Schley street Newark New Jersey 07112.

I also want to keep you in prayers send me your prayer request

MIRACLE OF GOD MINISTRIES INC
343 Sanford avenue
Newark New Jersey 07106

Also send in your generous donation to support this work at
www.fnabaziehealingministries.org

Chapter 2 : The Power of Dedication & Focus

CONCLUSION

"And Solomon determined to build an house for the name of the Lord, and an house for his kingdom.**2chr2:2**

"But I keep under my body, and bring it into subjection: lest that by any means, when I have preached to others, I myself should be a castaway." 1cor9:27

"Therefore if any man be in Christ, he is a new creature: old things are passed away; behold, all things are become new". 2cor5:17

Now repeat this Prayer after me

Say Lord Jesus, I accept you today, as my Lord and my savior, forgive me of my sins wash me with your blood. Right now, I believe, I am sanctified, I am save, I am free, I am free from the Power of sin to serve the Lord Jesus. Thank you Lord for saving me.

Amen. Congratulation: YOU ARE NOW A BORN AGAIN CHRISTAIN

What must I do to determine my divine visitation?

To determine divine visitation you must be born again! The word says as many as received him, to them gave He power to become the sons of God. Even to them that believe on his name.

To qualify for divine visitation do the following sincerely

1) Acknowledge that you are a sinner and that He died for you.Rom3:23.

2) Repent of your sins. Acts 3:19, Luke13:5, 2Peter3:9

3) Believe in your heart that Jesus died for your sin.Romans10:10

4) Confess Jesus as the Lord over your life. Romans10:10, Acts2:21

Chapter 2 : The Power of Dedication & Focus

Now repeat this Prayer after me

Say Lord Jesus, I accept you today, as my Lord and my savior, forgive me of my sins wash me with your blood. Right now, I believe, I am sanctified, I am save, I am free, I am free from the Power of sin to serve the Lord Jesus. Thank you Lord for saving me. Amen.

Join us on our weekly and Sunday worship services at 343 Sanford Avenue Newark New Jersey 07106. It's your season of laughter and new beginning.

The Power of Discipline & Dedication

I want to hear from you again. Please feel free to write me

REV FRANKLIN N ABAZIE
33 Schley street Newark
New Jersey 07112

OR

MIRACLE OF GOD MINISTRIES INC
343 SANFORD AVENUE NEWARK
NEW JERSEY 07106
Jesus is Lord.

EMAIL: Pastorfranknto@yahoo.com
Website www.fnabaziehealingministries.org

Chapter 2 : The Power of Dedication & Focus

WISDOM KEYS

Every Productive Society is a society heading to the top

Millions of Nigerians run away from Nigeria, very few Nigerians stay in Nigeria.

My decision to return Nigeria is the will of God for my life

My short coming in America after 18 years, trained me to be wise, to think, reflect and reason appropriately.

If you train your mind to reason it will train your hands to earn money.

It is absurd to use the money of the heathen to build the kingdom of the living God.

Every Ministry reveals its agenda and goal either at the beginning or at the end. Be careful of your life it is your first Ministry.

The Power of Discipline & Dedication

The average American mind is conditioned for a continual quest to get new things and (discard the former) and throw away old things.

When I considered well, my BMW jeep became my initial deposit for the work of the ministry in Nigeria

Everyone is waiting for you to change your mind until you change your thinking nothing changes around you.

Multiple academic degrees in other discipline gave me the chance to think, reflect, and reason

What so everyone are thinking and reflecting at the moment reveals you to the time and the now factor

All events and intents are the product of precise thought processes, accurate reason every event is designed for a designated timeline

Chapter 2 : The Power of Dedication & Focus

Wisdom is your ability to think, to create and invent. If you can think wise enough you will come out of penury

The distance between you and success is your creative ability to think reason and reflect accurate.

Success is the result of hard work, commitment resolve, and determination, learning from past mistakes and failing.

If you organize your mind you have organized your life and destiny.

There is a thin line between success and failure. If you look above and beyond you are on your way to success.

Wealth is your ability to think, power is your ability to reason and success is your ability to be informed.

The Power of Discipline & Dedication

If you can make use of your mind by thinking and reasoning God will make use of your life and destiny.

Think and Be Great

Reflect, Reason, think and be great

Famous people are born of woman

That you will make it is your intention; that you will survive is your resolve, that you will succeed with changes is your determination, personal efforts and hard work.

No man was born a failure. Lack of vision is the end product of failure.

Working with mental patients encourages and aspire me to be a productive observant and dedicated to my assignment.

Successful people are not magicians, it is the will power combined with hard work, and determination and a resolve to succeed that make them succeed.

Chapter 2 : The Power of Dedication & Focus

In the unequivocal state of the mind, intention is not a location or a position it is the state of the mind.

So many people think that they think. The mind is used to think reflect and reason. You will remain blind with your eye open until you can see with your mind by thinking.

There is no favoritism in accurate and precise calculation

Although knowledge is power, information is the key and gateway to a great future.

It will take the hand of God to move the hand of man.

With the backing of the great wise God, nothing will disconnect you from your inheritance.

As long as you have wisdom and understanding of God, Satan and evil cannot manipulate your life and destiny.

The Power of Discipline & Dedication

You have come this far by yourself judgment and decision you have made in the past, now lean and listen to God for another dimension of greatness.

Great people are common people it is extra ordinary effort and the price of sacrifice that produces greatness.

As a mental direct care worker I saw a great pastor and a motivational speaker within myself.

Menial job does not reduce your self-worth, until you resolve to achieve greatness see greatness in all you do; you will never count in your community.

The principle of Jesus will solve your gambling and addiction problems

The man of Jesus will lead you into heaven,

Everyone have their self-appraisal and what they think about you. Until you discover

Chapter 2 : The Power of Dedication & Focus

yourself other opinion about you will alter the real you.

Supervisors and directors are just a position in the chain of command in a work place. Never allow your supervisor hierarchy to alter your opinion about yourself.

Everyone can come out of debt if they make up their mind.

That I am not a decision maker at work does not diminish my contribution to my world.

Although it appears like it was a poor decision to accept a direct care employment at a psychiatric hospital as I reflect of my nine years of experience, it became apparent that I have learnt and experienced enough for my next assignment.

Self-encouragement and determination is a resolve of the heart.

The Power of Discipline & Dedication

If you are determined to make a difference, and do the things that make a difference you will eventually make a difference.

Good things do not come easy

Short cuts will cut your life short.

Those who look ahead move ahead.

Life is all about making an impact. In your life time strive to make an impact in your community.

Make friends and connect with people who are moving ahead of you in life.

If you can look around well you have come a long way in your life, made a lot of difference and realized a lot of success in life.

If you are my old friend, hurry up to reach out to me before I become a stranger to you.

Chapter 2 : The Power of Dedication & Focus

Everything I am blessed with inspirations from God, that change my definition and interpretation of the world around me.

I thought I was stagnant and lonely until I looked around and noticed my children running around and my wife cooking.

At 40 I resigned my Job to seek the Lord forever.

My ministry took a drastic rise to the top when the wisdom of God visited me with knowledge and understanding.

You will be a better person if you understand the characteristics of your personality – your mood swings attitudes and habits.

It is the seed of love you sow into the heart of a child and a woman that you reap in due time.

Love is not selfish, love share everything including the concealed secrets of the mind.

The Power of Discipline & Dedication

As long as you have a prayer life and a bible; you will never feel lonely, rejected, and idle in the race of life.

When good friends disconnect from you, let them go, they might have seen something new in a different direction.

Confidence in yourself and in God is the only way to bring you out of captivity

Never train a child to waste his/her time.

The mind is the greatest assets of a great future.

You walk by common sense run by principles and fly by instruction.

CHAPTER 3
PRAYER OF SALVATION

> "Neither is there salvation in any other: for there is none other name under heaven given among men, whereby we must be saved."
>
> **Acts4:12**

There is only one name that will take us all into heaven.

What must I do to determine my salvation?

To be saved we must be born again! The word says as many as received him, to them gave He power to become the sons of God. Even to them that believe on his name.

To qualify for divine visitation do the following sincerely

The Power of Discipline & Dedication

1) Acknowledge that you are a sinner and that
He died for you.Rom3:23.

2) Repent of your sins. Acts 3:19, Luke13:5, 2Peter3:9

3) Believe in your heart that Jesus died for your sin.Romans10:10

4) Confess Jesus as the Lord over your life. Romans10:10, Acts2:21

Now repeat this Prayer after me

Say Lord Jesus, I accept you today, as my Lord and my savior, forgive me of my sins wash me with your blood. Right now, I believe, I am sanctified, I am save, I am free, I am free from the Power of sin to serve the Lord Jesus. Thank you Lord for saving me. Amen. Congratulation: YOU ARE NOW A BORN AGAIN CHRISTIAN

Chapter 3 : Prayer of Salvation

AGAIN I SAY TO YOU CONGRATULATION

I adjure you to watch the Spirit of God bear witness with your Spirit confirming His word with signs following. The word says The Spirit itself beareth witness with our spirit, that we are the children of God..

MIRACLE CARE OUTREACH

"…But that the members should have the same care one for another" **1cor12:25**

We are all members of the body of Christ. Jesus commanded us to love our neighbor as ourselves. This includes caring for one another as a member of one body. True love is expressed in caring and giving. The word says for God so Love He gave….

Reach out to someone in need of Jesus, help someone in crisis find Christ. Look out and prove your love to Jesus by caring and inviting your friends and associates to find Jesus the Healer.

Invite your friends to our Home Care Cell Fellowship (Miracle chapel Intl Satellite fellowship) In the USA at 33 Schley Street Newark New Jersey 07112.

If you are in Nigeria—**MIRACLE OF GOD MINISTRIES**

A.K.A**"MIRACLE CHAPEL INTL"** Mpama –Egbu-Owerri Imo state Nigeria.

(Home Care Cell fellowship Group). We meet every Tuesday at 6:00pm-7:00pm.

LIFE IS NOT ALL ABOUT DURATION BUT ITS ALL ABOUT DONATION

What does the above statement mean?….

Life consists not in accumulation of material wealth. (Luke12:15) But it's all

Chapter 3 : Prayer of Salvation

about liberality....meaning- what you can give and share with others. Proverb11:25. When you live for others--You live forever- because you out live your generation by the legacy you live behind after you depart into glory to be with the Lord. But when you live to yourself - you are reduced to self—you are easily forgotten when you die and depart in glory. Permit me to admonish you today to live your life to be a blessing to a soul connected to you today. I want you to know that so many souls are connected and looking up to you, and through you so many souls will be saved and rescued from destruction. Will you disciple someone today to find Jesus Christ?

As a genuine Christian; it is your duty to evangelize Jesus Christ to all you meet on your way. Jesus is still in the healing business-Jesus is still doing miracles from time of old to now. Therefore tell someone about Jesus Christ today, disciple and bring them to Church. John 1:45 *Philip findeth Nathanael....*

Please to prove the sincerity of your love for God today; please become a soul winner. The dignity of your Christianity is hidden in your boldness to proclaim and evangelize Jesus Christ to all you meet on your way. There is a question mark on the integrity of your Christianity until you become a life soul winner. Invite someone to join us worship the Lord Jesus this coming Sunday. **Amen**

MIRACLE OF GOD MINISTRIES PILLARS OF THE COMMISSION

We Believe Preach and Practice the following

1) We believe and preach Salvation to every living human being

2) We believe and preach Repentance and forgiveness of sins

Chapter 3 : Prayer of Salvation

3) We believe and preach the baptism of the Holy Spirit and Spiritual gifts

4) We believe and teach the Prosperity

5) We believe and preach Divine Healing and Miracles (Signs &Wonder)

6) We believe and preach Faith

7) We believe and Proclaim the Power of God (Supernatural)

8) We believe and Proclaim Praise& Worship to God

9) We believe and preach Wisdom

10) We believe and preach Holiness (Consecration)

11) We believe and preach Vision

12) We believe and teach the Word of God

13) We believe and teach Success

14) We believe and practice Prayer

15) We believe and teach Deliverance

The Power of Discipline & Dedication

This 15 stones form the Pillars of Our Commission. Become part of this church family and follow this great move of God.

MY HEART FELT PRAYER FOR YOU

It is my prayer that you testify today about the goodness of the Lord. I desire for you to have an encounter with our Lord Jesus Christ.

Now let me Pray for you:

Our Father in Heaven, I pray for the release of your power to be discipline. Power to be devoted, dedicated, and hardworking in anything we set our eyes to accomplish in life. Father Lord be with us and strengthen us in a unique way. I thank you in advance for you have done upon my life. In Jesus Mighty name **Amen.**

Chapter 3 : Prayer of Salvation

THE POWER OF EVANGELISM

"Go ye therefore, and teach all nations, baptizing them in the name of the Father, and of the Son, and of the Holy Ghost:" **Mathew28:19**

Evangelism has power to attract the blessing of the Lord upon our lives. It is written "And ye shall serve the Lord your God, and he shall bless thy bread, and thy water; and I will take sickness away from the midst of thee." **Exodus23:26.**

Evangelizing, and bringing men and women to the cross of Jesus Christ is a great commandment. According to the above scripture, we are commanded to teach all nations, the name of Jesus Christ.

It is my prayer that you will witness the name of Jesus Christ to someone today.

Remember………..

"And they that be wise shall shine as the brightness of the firmament; and they that turn many to righteousness as the stars for ever and ever." **Daniel 12:3**

OPERATION--"ONE MAN TEN MEN"

"Thus saith the Lord of hosts; In those days it shall come to pass, that ten men shall take hold out of all languages of the nations, even shall take hold of the skirt of him that is a Jew, saying, We will go with you: for we have heard that God is with you." **Zecharia 8:23**

If someone directed you to this ministry, it is divine wisdom for you to bring someone else also. If you googled to come into contact with us, I will recommend you also tell ten of your contacts and share with them what Jesus is doing through this ministry.

Chapter 3 : Prayer of Salvation

Tell everybody about Jesus, also tell them to contact this ministry. Jesus is Lord!!

OPERATION ONE MAN ONE SOUL

If you cannot bring ten people at one time, at least you can talk to one person per time.

I recommend that you look for just one person who will respond positively and bring them to church. Or tell them about this ministry. That convert, is your own convert minister to them the love of Jesus Christ.

JESUS IS LORD!

CHAPTER 4
ABOUT THE AUTHOR

Rev Franklin N Abazie is the founding and Presiding Pastor of Miracle of God Ministries with headquarters in Newark, New Jersey USA and a branch church in Owerri- Imo State Nigeria. He is following the footsteps of one of his mentors, Oral Roberts (Healing Evangelist) of the blessed memory. The Lord passed Oral Roberts healing mantle two days before he went to be with the Lord at age 91 into the hand of healing evangelist-Rev Franklin N Abazie in a vision.

In all his services the Power and Presence of God is present to heal all in his audience. He is an ordained man of God with a Healing Ministry reviving the healing and miracle ministry of Jesus Christ of Nazareth.

Chapter 4 : About The Author

Pastor Franklin N Abazie, is called by God with a unique mandate: **"THE MOMENT IS DUE TO IMPACT YOUR WORLD THROUGH THE REVIVAL OF THE HEALING & MIRACLE MINISTRY OF JESUS CHRIST OF NAZARETH**

I AM SENDING YOU TO RESTORE HEALTH UNTO THEE AND I WILL HEAL THEE OF THY WOUNDS. SAID THE LORD OF HOST"

He is a gifted ardent Teacher of the word of God who operates also in the office of a Prophet, generating and attracting undeniable signs & wonders, special miracles and healings, with apostolic fireworks of the Holy Ghost. He is the founding and presiding senior Pastor of this fast growing Healing ministry. He has written over 86 inspirational, healing and transforming books covering almost all aspect of divine healing and life. He is happily married and blessed with children.

BOOKS BY REV FRANKLIN N ABAZIE

1) Commanding Abundance
2) The outcome of faith
3) Understanding the secret of prevailing prayers.
4) Understanding the secret of the man God uses
5) Activating my due Season
6) Overcoming Divine Verdicts
7) The Outcome of Divine Wisdom
8) Understanding God's Restoration Mandate
9) Walking in the Victory and Authority of the truth
10) Gods Covenant Exemption
11) Destiny Restoration Pillars

12) Provoking Acceptable Praise
13) Understanding Divine Judgment
14) Activating Angelic Re-enforcement
15) Provoking Un-Merited Favor
16) The Benefits of the Speaking faith
17) Understanding Divine Arrangement
18) Understanding Divine Healing
19) The Mystery of Endurance
20) Obeying Divine Instructions
21) Understanding the Voice of God
22) Never give up on Hope
23) The prevailing Power of faith
24) Understanding Divine Prosperity
25) The Reward of Prayer
26) Covenant Keys to Answered Prayers
27) Activating the Forces of Vengeance

Books by Rev Franklin N Abazie

28) Put your faith to work
29) Where is your trust?
30) The Audacity of the Blood of Jesus
31) Redeeming Your Days
32) The Force of Vision
33) Breaking the shackles of Family curses
34) Wisdom for Marriage Stability
35) Overcoming prevailing challenges
36) The Prayer solution
39) The power of Prayer
40) Prayer strategy
41) The prayer that works
42) Walking in Forgiveness
43) The Power of the grace of God
44) The Power of Persistence
45) Overcoming Divine verdicts

46) The benefit of the speaking faith.

47) Fearless faith

48) Redeeming Your Days.

49) The Supernatural Power of Prophecy

50) The companionship of the Holy Spirit

51) Understanding Divine Judgement

52) Understanding Divine Prosperity

53) Dominating Controlling Forces

54) The winner's Faith

55) Destiny Restoration Pillars

56) Developing Spiritual Muscles

57) Inexplicable faith

58) The lifestyle of Prayer

59) Developing a positive attitude in life.

60) The Mystery of Divine supply

61) Encounter with the Power of God

Books by Rev Franklin N Abazie

62) Walking in love

63) Praying in the Spirit

64) How to provoke your testimony

65) Walking in the reality of the anointing

66) The Reality of new birth

67) The Price of freedom

68) The Supernatural Power of faith

69) The intellectual components of Redemption.

70) Overcoming Fear

71) Overcoming Prevailing Challenges

72) My life & Ministry

73) The Mystery of Praise

MIRACLE OF GOD MINISTRIES

*NIGERIA CRUSADE
2012*

MIRACLE OF GOD MINISTRIES

NIGERIA CRUSADE
2012

MIRACLE OF GOD MINISTRIES

*NIGERIA CRUSADE
2012*

www.ingramcontent.com/pod-product-compliance
Lightning Source LLC
Chambersburg PA
CBHW030059100526
44591CB00008B/204